Advance Praise for

All Brown Boys Get Trumpets

"Matthew 'Cuban' Hernandez's poems are an anthem of resilience. He writes about grief with unflinching tenderness and reverence. In a world that doesn't often give men the opportunity to be flawed and vulnerable, Hernandez offers a masterclass in being human. He describes himself as having an unquenchable thirst for love, and in *All Brown Boys Get Trumpets*, the reader will also embrace this beautiful thirst. Matthew Hernandez has lovingly used this poetry collection to teach Brown Boys to master flight one jump at a time, a calling for all of us misfits to soar."

—Yesika Salgado, author of *Corazón*, *Tesoro*, and *Hermosa*

"Matthew 'Cuban' Hernandez is the kind of writer who makes you want to live bigger. You'll be going about your day and something will remind you of a poem of his and the moment will exponentially expand through the lens of his words. I'm grateful for his perspective, his extraordinary ability to articulate it, and this new collection of little windows into his world, and in turn, ours as well."

—JP Saxe, Grammy nominated singer-songwriter

"*All Brown Boys Get Trumpets* is such a gift. Like a tapestry, the poems seamlessly interweave threads of childhood and identity, blessings, and folklore, hopes and regrets. Never before has a book felt more like an heirloom to me--something hard-earned and sunkissed and meant to be cherished."

—Sierra DeMulder, internationally-acclaimed author, poet, healer and host of podcast "Just break up"

"Matthew Cuban has always been and will always be a poet among the people."

—G YAMAZAWA, artist

All Brown Boys Get Trumpets

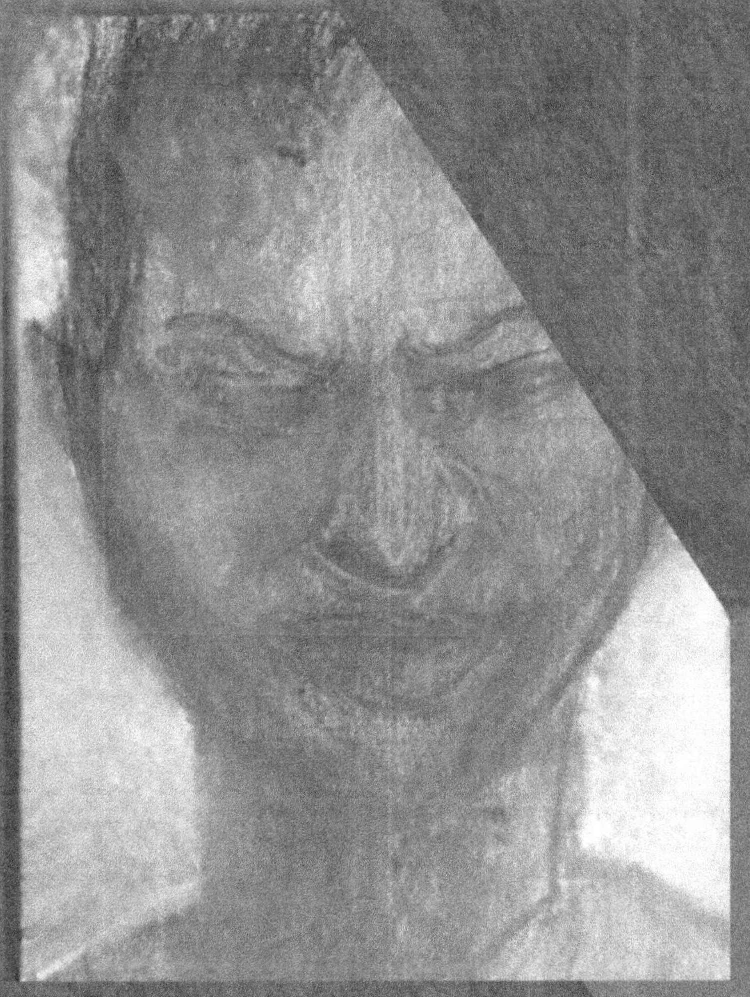

MATTHEW CUBAN HERNANDEZ

ISBN: 979-8-8693-0757-6

Published by El Martillo Press
in the United States of America.
elmartillopress.com

Cover art by Robalu Gibsun.

Set in Poppins.
Typeset for El Martillo Press by Matthew 'Cuban' Hernandez
and David A. Romero.

Edited by Alyesha Wise-Hernandez and Theo DeMarco.

NOTICE: SCHOOLS AND BUSINESSES
El Martillo Press offers copies of this book at quantity discount
with bulk purchase for educational, business, or sales
promotional use. For information, please email the publisher
at elmartillopress@gmail.com.

Table of Contents

This book is dedicated to every kid told who they were, before discovering on their own. It's for the teachers and mentors praying their students won't fall into the traps the world has set for them. These poems are for liberation, and those who strive for peace by any means. For the ones who feel like a mistake, the ones riddled with grief and self-doubt. This book is for Duval County and every poet who inspired me to believe that dreams come true. For every undiagnosed genius believing their words aren't worth reading. This book is for grief. This is for Ivanna, for Pablo, for Olga, for Emma, for Tonya, for Will, for Clinton, for Samantha, for Reddin, every ancestor at my back and their shoulders I stand on. This is for anyone who's ever had someone yuck their yum. I promise you're already amazing.

So much in my heart
I curtain call my grateful
Here I am, smiling

Baby Mustache

The brown boy receives a trumpet
melodies for tears

the brown boy learns strength
in prayers for survival

the brown boy plays just to play, his joy
a weapon, an instrument waiting
a tool repurposed, repossessed
birthed to take sadness and rupture ears

who listens
then calls their noise a knotting
what sound does a brown boy make
without a vessel to breathe life into
baby mustache, seen adult before teen
brown boys at the border seen men now too
or expected to be, accountable
but who keeps track when a brown boy goes
missing, in the oven of their bodies
in an unfamiliar mirror, and the family
doesn't notice the vanishing
when he still shows up in photographs
how can you be sure he left at all
when his giggle a whaling mistaken for delight
his notes too high with head held low

they give the brown boy a trumpet
when an option was requested
others know what's best

know family, and God, and school
and chores, and anything
before healing
before listening to a brown boy's
wants and fears, he's handed a stereotype
told make it beautiful
a long-lost relative never met
voluntelling you what to learn
and somehow a brown boy's hands become
a perfect fit, somehow
he learns to love his hand-me-downs
a work ethic born from necessity
he learned from his parents
a melody hummed in the blood
of every ancestor

                    I tell myself I'm lucky, I was given my identity
                          as a name, turned my story into a poem
                      learned every chapter in life is an evolving
                            learned my blessing as an obligation
                                       fulfilled in classrooms
                           full of brown boys, written off
                           by a world that wants them silent
                                    I open my life like a map
                           we're both learning to read

            Raymond tell me he used to be
                 in marching band

me too, what'd you play

                                        the trumpet

me too

                    yeah, all brown boys get trumpets

and we chuckle
both knowing the joke
was on us

Greatness

Someone said jump
I began to fly
someone said stop
and I built a bunker to collapse
into, I once listened to someone
once ran for someone's opinion
before tearing mine from a book
I was writing instead of reading
someone said to love myself, too
and at that moment, anything anyone
told me became a protest, a chance
for my voice, my option or opinion or onion
unraveling itself to tears, someone said,
love life, live love, and everything I hoped for
became drywall, became a swimming
pool of grief, and moments I said no
when I should have thought *evolve*, or
I should have said *ok*

I'm here
    I'm on my way
I'm sorry
    I'm sorry
I'm so sorry, I'll live with this forever
if you ever

      someone once said, "devil emoji"
said I'm flailing, I'm failings
and this time, you can do nothing

but watch

on the shoreline of eternity

        I once heard a poem start like that

or was it
        on the shoreline of my indiscretions

not sure, though
something sure is powerful about the shore
"she sells seashells by the seashore"
Pauly Shore
    hilarious in the 90's
        when all things problematic flourished
sure, you right

"shore" sure feels like the word
        "stop"
      feels like an end
of a lineage, or a cycle
or
   life

I've stood at edges of oceans
around the world, thinking in circles
mindful moments
imagining a life 30 years from now

but I guess the ocean makes you think
the shore feels like a ticket booth
to dreaming, a concession stand for imagination
letting the sun and salt air whisper
centuries of lullabies, letting all that we don't know
become a memory to retell
a legacy to write, and rewrite and set
adrift, off the shore of every indiscretion
a time loop constantly asking,

what do you truly want in this wide world

when action is more important than words
at times, because a thought can stall
                momentum
                        because fear
                            because now
                                because now
                                    because right now
in this moment, the only
greatness I know is a child writing
about her depression, writing about being sad
and allowing her words to become a song
the entire class sings

at times, all I want to be is an eraser
at times, all I want to be is a ceremony
an atom bomb, or something terrible enough
to be taken seriously, to be what survives
what grows after the rubble
after the building
        and rebuilding
            and rewriting
                and reworking
                    and working
                        and working
                            and still

become an opening
of a hand, a gentle drag to warmth
to sun, to grow
to glow and
shimmer

Sutured Heart

Beyond blood and bone
a book of poems named *home*,
a curtain to hide your smiles in

beyond blood and bone
a sweltering place to roam
a balled dome wishing wax
to shine its smile upon

beyond blood and bone
a bulging bulb shining hotter
than a sun never done or finished
growing from times diminished
and smiles in all the darkest places

beyond blood and bone
bold, writing cold, like a grin
in the snow, or opening
to a show

beyond blood and bone could be alone

                    could be

could be alone

                but

chooses to be around,
never square, just a smile

shining in the waxing of a moon
or a shadow in the sky

beyond blood and bone
is a clone of my greatness
a warm hug's waiting

how else could we have made it
wading in the riptide of life
we've been placed in

it's beyond blood or bone
it's the trust we give and the trust that implodes
it's open hands clasped together
a prayer you don't remember, whispering
meaningless moments that mean everything
when they are the last

beyond blood and bone
my mother sits
beyond this world, and still
a tidal force, a guiding spirit, a waning lament
birthed through poem
like suturing heart, with appellation

Thorns

My joy

breaking bread
breaking cycles
building trust
trusting spirit

trusting ancestors
knowing myself
self-loving feverishly

the choice of joy
the act of joy

it's finding
when the world is a gut
punch

loving the thorns
                    learning what is around you
including
                    understanding the traps
clearing the mess
            knowing what is built for you, or
built to destroy you

                        reconstructing your foundation

loving your lonely
                        appreciating your weird

finding your gift

and giving it to everyone

Olga's Voice

Deep down I am still a child
looking for candy to steal
convincing myself
I deserve, what I did not earn

tenderness
discernment
a second chance

shame

pretending, passing through
the motions until the weekend
or the next time I can sleep
without guilt

deep down I am still
a child alone in a house
on the corner of Third and Dena
in a hood called Paxson
where siblings and I learned hard lessons
to clean the dirt off scraped knees
and walk off our bruising
even when sprouting sadness

buried in my youth
the brightest memories beam
an event horizon spaghettifying
laughter into what we forget
and what we cannot

like the smell
of my mother's hair
or the sound
of my grandmother singing
often, loud
and awful
and how beautiful

fuck it can really sound

Crossing Doubt

What is hope
a flower
not in bloom
a fist
unable to uncurl

what is hope
another breath
ashamed inspiration
in privacy
a small thing I can carry
in my palm
without crushing

a beginning
yet to start
and an ending
named anything but
fear

Faith-Fully

Begin with a yawn
        pop
           a snap of joints
        my immaturity rusting over

I breathe
a gasp for crisp air
embracing my mourning

faithfully, I'm a pillow
too warm to stay
awake for

                a drifting place, or

I'm enthralled in what gives me moments
to float
from yesterday
so, I begin

with ambition, a longing a
yearning as if
I could fit tighter
        in a world desperate to splinter me out

so, begin with clasped hands
        fingers interlaced
           like a universal palindrome
                starting where I end
              and ending where I begin

grieving, between the life I've lived
and moments that gave me reason

Vacancy

The grateful in me
wants to be quiet
wants to hold my warmth
inside a cabin, feels
guilty when I speak
about my joy, it's more precious
than food

the grateful in me knows
people are starving for more
than food, knows this world
could snap at the break
of a newsfeed, or our new favorite show

the grateful in me has its arms full
hands outstretched to catch myself
to hold everything up and in
to keep it together, for everyone else
to realize the grateful in my belly laughs
the way it steals my breath
like sprinting into your arms

the grateful in me has 57 pictures
of my mother

the grateful in me says ,
that's more than some

the grateful in me cries
at night

when no one's around
when my pain can only hurt myself
my gratitude closes eyes

I get scared
and think
of losing more, losing everything
and everyone
I think of cards built on sand
sleeping with clenched fists
and jaw and breath
fingers latched tight around my blanket
and awaken to so much grateful
more than enough, an over abundance
so much more than these arms
could ever carry

Submerged

I circle the drain of my want
I curve and cruise the angel's choice
I call invitation out of fear of calling it fate
I am both scared and sacred

the difference, I cannot tell

I curl into a halo
I call my crown a man bun
I curl my fear into a ball and roll it into a corner
I circle back to preadolescence ignored

until I am a moment
impossible to bring back

I circle myself, pray ancestors
show me meaning
I find reason, in the gust of my grief
I hear her daily, not always in words
I still wish that was enough

The Fix

I'm a charged controller
and a drained spirit

I'm fresh food
and spoiled patience

a friend holding happy
like a ticket

I'm an overbooked calendar
and the anxiety of stagnation

I'm running late
or way too early

spinning and wishing
for a moment to steady

I'm half-drunk
cups of coffee

a full glass
of the snooze button
and fuck off

disheveled living room,
dusty paint-chipped
everything

a flickering light or
more things needing
to be fixed

I am the fix

                                        and the broken

              and my glue game is tight
              my welds are getting better
              and I am so phosphorus
              most nights I beam
              without trying

Knowing

What do you fear will happen
when you open your palms
like a storm drain
and finally push out all the mess
of not knowing

what do you think will happen
when you can't see what happens
when you can't predict
the asteroid of honesty
just waiting
hurtling through space
for a civilization to level
or love into yesterday's dust

do you remember being love
or loved, or what
do you think will
happen, when all your lonely
finally leaves

Perra

There is a dog In me
a loyal happy fool waiting
for someone to pat
my head and let me destroy
their furniture
there is a dog in me, a backwards
God, barking for its supper
while expecting to keep guard
on an empty stomach, there is
a dog in me, chasing the cars of my desires
afraid of what will, or won't happen
when I catch it, there is a dog in me, a golden
German Shepherd or a pit bull named Yogi
who grew into a mut, instead of a good prince
a good dog either way
the dog in me, dreams
of leading a pack, dreams of running and
running and never looking
back to find home, there
is a dog in me wondering if he'll ever
find a way home
or if all the color of the world is just shades of--
the dog in me is scared of lightning
the dog in me digs and
digs, and buries nothing
but the urge to dig, there is a dog in me
and he's just a dog, not a descendant of wild
but the embodiment of joy
every moment

awake, another chance
to attack the day or your shadow
chasing your tail
with a permanent
panting grin

Stalling

When death comes
I'mma be like, *(shit)*
no matter how much time I've used
I'll still be "Stalin" like Joseph
still making deals to loiter longer
like lines of poetry left to linger
until written into existence

I'll be all like, *cool cool cool*
then take off running, or
throw a punch, or a tantrum

I'll be like, *hold up, I need to finish*
this one thing, I gotta call this... I gotta
make sure they remember that moment
everything changed, I gotta
mark every pitfall, roadmap my happiness
so, all who come after know
why, and how, I smiled so often

when death comes
I'll make it coffee, I'll make it
wait, and wait, for every time I said, *now* or *today*
my story in my hands, a crumpled bible
taking myself out
to dinner, like a last meal
I'll offer my death dinner, I'll sing
what being alive has taught me

ask it to stay overnight

knowing it'll be gone with the sun

when death comes, honestly
I'll be like
oh yeah, this is how I go
and I'll go
because I'll want to
with ancestors holding open doors
I don't think I'll feel undone
after spending a lifetime in love
with everyone

when death comes
I'm sure it'll be my mom
it won't feel like I'm gone
just finally welcomed home

with all I love a memory
and all my words
a poem

Pericardium II

A pulsing life
a flashing light
that's my whole
right there
my complete rotation
my finished, my findings
that's my heart right there
my smile, my full belly, my exhausted
rest, my rest, my all, my every-
-thing, that's it right there

a paper becoming
testimony, becoming triumph, becoming
and unbecoming, be the arrival
the changing, be chanting, be worship
be beauty, still be broken
can't be beauty without
broken, can't be a painting
without shards of *almost*, and that's my home
right there
my prayer to air, with no response
my false flame, Wizard of Oz hidden
behind a curtain, that's my power
right there
my poems right there, my love
my heart, right here
right here, right here

Blessings

After Lucille Clifton and Tonya Ingram

Blessings to all that tried to kill me
and failed
blessings to failures of killing myself
the long nights, the open road
whose swallow I escaped
the hometown that chewed and spit out
friends like sunflower seeds
blessings to childhood goals, the NFL I never
came close to, for the 3rd place and the forgotten

blessings to gossip, the untruths
clambering for acceptance
the hungry depression, never satisfied
never full, wanting my community
and my company, the gnarled dog in the corner
of my tidy home, the home I keep clean
in place of a college diploma
praise to the public school
the hood and the impostor syndrome it bundles

blessings to the strays
animals wandering for home
the times I lead the herd, the times
I was the pack
blessings to the push, to not giving up or in
to the days I fight to feel the sun's heat
the days that only know the countdown
until the next, identities worn like face paint

covering scars

blessings to the writers
ones who never learned to translate
self-love but heard it in their voice
blessings to tomorrow, how it arrives
how it arrives, how it sits with
impossible, until you awake
to the knocking
blessings to the now, how it begs
to be lived in
how it never pulls for your attention
but always deserves it

Overboard of Education

A child
sun of words and
      warmth
love
  set
    adrift
                  an unforgiving ocean
tiny ship
      no life preserver
rising and lowering
      with the crest of waves
barely holding on
     barely
keeping water out
of lungs
alone

an empty sea   sharks circling
how many
      started out
        from the shore
saying, *I hope he comes back*
          hope he doesn't drown
few set themselves to search

no voice to speak back, no
            temper to calm
      no housing to find
no help to give

no opportunities to shift direction
no saving
no speech

no amount of money or time
a missed mark, a passing
comet, a star flickering in sight
but long since turned cold

would it have made a difference
unable to unearth his wreckage
will the ones who found themselves lost
against the tide, find their way home

how many students can be held
in the eye of a hurricane, sink
or swim, but everyone I know is barely
treading water
sink or swim, but we don't
float, keeping our lips
perched, almost breaking
the surface, gasping for air
grasping for healing
like hands
holding water

Fisherman

The neighborhood forgets their face

        wandering a field of stubborn

                an ocean of warped adolescence

a knot untended

      a light, soft and gentle, asking to reach

                the darkest parts of the city–

the hood memorialized behind eyelids,

      no safety, rehabilitation, or enforcement

just numbers,

        organized, categorized

                stored and incarcerated

My Heart, My Shell

Born a conch shell
born a sea turtle
born a rock, or a hard place
or boat
born a brick
built like a wall
something made up to keep out, or in
to suppress
to surprise
or tear down
born like a bullhorn
a siren wailing
a calling or culling
to the war machines
under our collarbones
bones like shells, slugs or shields
armored fragments shuffling under the skin
the parts we wear like car paint
chrome covering the dings and dents
from existing in this unkind place
born like a bullet
born like gunshot
or ricochet
born like a battle cry
but not born to cry
or deconstruct the bricks our ancestors created
to keep us alive
even if we were just a thought
or a dream

even if we'd never find out
or know
even if all we get for their construction
is air in our lungs
still born a shell casing
still built like a boomerang
coming back to the things that pushed
us the furthest away. still spinning
moving, but only in circles. still
protecting our fragile like it's not the strongest
part of our resolve
like it's not our greatest resource
disguised as a wilting rose
like it's not the only part of my mother
I can still feel and speak to, and speak from
like I wasn't
born with a to-do list
like I wasn't built to grow from this lineage of trauma

like I wasn't the trauma
like I wasn't the growth
like I'm not growing, existing for the lives no longer able to live
like I'm not just a chip off the old block. the old shell
talkin 'bout *you need me*
talkin 'bout I'm weak
without the comfort I hide behind
talking 'bout, *I'm good*
saying, *you good bro bro*
just sleep
just rest
just stay tired and call it productive
call it busy or distraction or destruction, call it
the bones or walls
call it an ugly shield
call it a bullhorn
singing the map you'll follow
all the way to home

all the way to heart

Clumsy Panting

Sometimes
my imagination is a burning house
the fire lit inside
the windows flicker flames
lapping like tongues, struggling taste
at times, my imagination is a stunted toddler
caught in the excitement of just existing
picky and fidgety, a true Gemini,
both desperately needing attention
while craving alone time

at times, my imagination is an old dog
about 15 in human years but geriatric
for its species, it lumbers around my home
waits for me to finish my work
waits for me to feed it
waits for me to acknowledge its existence
then put it to sleep, and
isn't that what happens
to all unused imagination
laid to rest
put down, out of its misery, ignored
when begging for life, and mourned
the moment
its clumsy panting
can no longer be heard

One Day

On the day my body carries memories
like bags of sand, and time
is a boiling sea, bulging
for a final adventure, hopefully
I'll look back on right now and remember
that my problems were only puzzles
my anger only a shadow
pretending monster, and everything is
as it was always
maybe I'll be playing some video games
feeling ageless, like time
and life will go on forever
maybe I'll be surrounded by children or poets
sad faces trying to turn every moment
into eternity, and I'll laugh
kiss their hands and their foreheads
I'll whisper something
like, *stop being so dramatic, don't you see me
in the babies, don't you hear me in their play
read my words, my heart could
never stay quiet*

Rest

The wicked need this too
none for those who dream
fantasy for those unsatisfied

the wicked need this too
a bundle of *believe*
fantasy for those burdened with their purpose
wrapped in self-love

a bundle of *believe*
we become what we deny
wrapped in love of self
clawing at what slips away

we become what we deny
the parents we've grown from
clawing at what slips away
and pretending we're fine

the parents we grow out of, then
become none for those who dream
and pretend everything is fine
when we rest

Taking the Wheel

We live in snapshot moments
letting chance determine greatness
they only happen when we own it
it's not if, it's when, stay patient

letting chance determine greatness
when time is the hungriest enemy
it's not if, it's when, stay patient
embracing what life has done to me

when time is the hungriest enemy
I prepared my day for war
embraced what life has done for me
not for death, this existence is more

I prepared myself for war
taking care with every second
not for death, this life is more
and the days that I've perfected

taking care with every second
they only happen when we own it
and the days that I've perfected
while living in snapshot moments

Deafening

When sound sets itself to still
the silence is devil, and
there is still so much sound
so, the silence is a demon
when only thoughts break the nothingness
only fear allowing itself an octave
the night sounds like the last time
I spoke to my mother

please don't cry, I'll be back in a few weeks

sounds like a lie

regret

a rusty ship taking on what it cannot keep out
my yesterday is a tetanus shot
I've refused to take
rest sounds like the tossing
and turning of sheets
heat pooling at the center
of my bed, the cold sweat never drying
to comfort, the roll of traffic
outside my window
building itself to morning rush
wailing sirens, the harbinger of
someone's awful day, the pulse
of everyone's frustration bellowing
into horns and growling engines
you don't hear *good morning*

just the urgency to get somewhere you hate
to live a life
the child in you would turn tantrum
over, I hear my life
amongst the instruments, the discord
it makes, the frequency it searches
or an echo
long since passed

In This Place

I remember the parts of myself
unblemished by fear
the sections untouched
left alone
to rust or mold over

I remember my spirit
a famished optimism, wanting nothing
but to be seen and nurtured
spoke constantly of what could be
if guilt wasn't carried like a suitcase
if doubt wasn't second language
if regret did hold memories
like a jealous lover

I remember
every time I said *no*
or *that's enough*
or *when will I change*
then fall into sadness
like a warm mattress, continuously made
to nest doubt, still

I remember her smile
his love
my responsibility
and all the reasons I can't
allow myself to breathe
I'll look back one day, and remember
the things I chose to plant and forget

like an unkempt garden of possibility
my fear seems
raindrops on a rose
to provide nourishment
help me grow
in ways that don't
feel like drowning

maybe the closer we flirt
with what can overwhelm
the more beautiful we bloom
my pain, an old friend too
young and full of life for forgetting
a daily plea, an unending exhaustion
whispers *give in, then give up*
but I found a glimmering smile, in this place
most anxious to leave, with a prayer

I will remain

I will prosper

Folklore

I try to be open
trying to capture moments in memory
like vaults I'll forget combinations to
trying to notice time, watching leaves
fall and grow back, then
drift to the ground again
watching my wife, taking special notice
of her smile, watch it grow
over ice cream or anything about aliens
I watch my cat, my apartment, the home
built from grit and love
opening myself to life and therefore
opening myself to loss
seeing beauty in this too
telling myself my mother's pain is
just a memory to lock away
that she is no longer
suffering, therefore, part of every good
in my life, watching
the beautiful manchild I've become
a curious mess of discoveries
my revaluation and revelations
so much room for *better*
enough for joy, love and patience
and what is beauty if freedom from self's hate
every decision becoming folklore
all possible, all answers

Made New

Let the tar of existence wash away
don't bleach or soak my skin
taking my color, my spices
bland and predictable
let this anger burn out
before engulfing intentions
let my body cinder to the last flicker
let me give in to possibility
before *all that could be* becomes myth
let me live my story like a dream
a script I don't remember writing
a hidden room in my childhood
a smile held in front like a shield
let all that is patently obvious
reveal itself from greening camouflage
let all who say they know
be given surprise
let the anxiety of what is new
be cradle in the arms of familiarity
let what needs to die, die
and new leaders be born
from mouths
of babies

Most Daze

I miss my mom
I felt guilty for

I feel like I could have extended her life
therefore, I feel like

she raised me, it shortened her life
with more love and patience than any god

sometimes the weight of this failure
seems insurmountable at night

I try to think only of her before I sleep
so, maybe I can apologize

in a dream, when I see her
I forget she's gone

it makes real life feel see-through
for the rest of my life

I don't need to wonder
I know I need help

to unload this burden
without the guilt

I miss my mother, but
almost 6 years have passed and

I can no longer grieve in public

I know that doesn't make sense

I know what I would tell my students
but this failure makes me

feel like a shame, doing anything
for her legacy

feels too little too late
maybe with time this weight will lighten
or I will

at least become strong enough
to live life, as a tribute to hers

Melodies

Heart, teach me patience, to hold
my excitement like beans in a pressure cooker
let my creative process mold into an
arroz con pollo of healing
to allow myself to feel then revive
the source of my strength
to bank the good days and compliments
for when I'm abandoned and frail
for when the hell I held back
braces for impact with all I call love

heart, teach me how to brace
to taste moments like fruit
and allow them to take root
to hold onto sand of my sorrow
in a raging river of time

heart, teach me to live
let me daily be my regular
let me *regular*
be you
be a smile
be a canvas made of giggles

heart, teach me how to survive
not to live but be alive
a tide pulling me to another
chance to spread what raised me
like paint spilling into the cracks and creaks
of my doubt

and I'll sing by answering the phone
being present when you are near
being alive while you are not
my melody is, thankful
life and all its dramas my heart wears

the wind pushing against denial
a gust compunction continuously blurring
my scrawlings to confetti

how many poems and books and stories
experiences, lifetimes, memories
will be forgotten

if feeling so much
was not meant to be written or read
then why feel anything at all
why let dread and blunder climb
the wallpaper of my every act
I have fed myself to a breeze
I am waiting to hear a song
I have tried to constitute many
yet many feel like the one
I've used to lullaby
myself asleep

Introduction

I'm brown boy
a man child
a grizzly hug
a misjudged cover
an unexpected ending
a new study
an old treat
a rabbit, a bottomless hat
a surprise can of beans
the corner bag of rice
the boil
the simmer, the seasonings
the ladle, the legacy
a pat on the back
a conversation worth having
that never happens
a family secret and curse
a cure, a harvest, a harness
a hailstorm, a journal
a couple months of rent
an empty checking account
*cómo se dice, saving*s

I'm a chuckle, a private message
I'm hidden in a look, a perfect place
or a poem about working on purpose

who am I
love
passed like heirlooms

a hug personified, when I smile
my ancestors introduce themselves
I am my family's wildest dreams
a river without an ocean
to end itself

I am my wife's silence
her belly laugh, underlying
conversations we have without words
I am the community that raised me
the Ritz Theatre in Duval County
streets where play was interrupted
by the passing of a car or classmate
by sun's setting, or the sounds of shots
a block over
that morning, my parents found a way
for the dinner they weren't sure
they could provide, maybe

I'm a yawn, an open mouth
some thought, a scream
a loose door looking at a lock
like a hieroglyph looking at closed door
like a window
I am my mother's spirit, the wisdom
she never tried for
the God she never grew out of
I am the Yoruba, the Afro-indigenous
the native and the namaste
the melting of history pretending itself
genetics, I am not yet
but soon to be

I am a waiting room
holding a number patiently
to be called

who am I

my mother's magic
my ancestors' wildest dreams
my family's story keeper
a wounded healer, a waiting hug
a present listener
an extended invitation
a warm home, a safe space
a driven leader and a focused student
a quad-racial mixed boy
with no one to resemble
when all my clay has molded
into a man with the world's smile
a gated grin, a bellowing laugh, who am I

beautiful
no caveat
just beautiful

and brilliant, brown and all these things
that bounce and shake and take
up space never built for boys like me
I am dreams standing behind paper barricades
daring to ignite, I am
my city's favorite son
a blade of grass on a field in Paxson
I am Fugie's gifted bike, gunfire during church

Fugie's last breath, Will's last breath
Tavis' last breath, Clinton's last breath
Pablo's last breath, Reddin's last breath
Samantha's last breath, Tessica's last breath
Rage's last breath, Tonya's last breath
Ivanna's breath, wisdom, magic

her magic
          her magic
                    her magic

her will to live

smirking at death while knocking at the door
smirking at doctors who only care
for 15 minutes at a time

I am becoming what I believe
and I believe I am enough

I am my own belief
and I believe that I am abundance

extra toppings on everything
dessert after seconds, after a second wind
a captured breath, a moment
immortalized, an unquenchable thirst for love
and love and learning and love and most
importantly who I am is just
getting started

West 3rd

Where I'm from, I learned to play
tackle football on concrete
busted knees, elbows, proof of time
well-spent, here, my Aunt Lourdes cooks
black beans, never a "side dish"
sustenance only her heart, hands and
becoming leftovers could make better
where I'm from, strays run the block
family gathers for a football team that
won't win, where the air is hot, humid
and everything smells like outside
where I'm from, Ivanna would tease
and Jorge strummed an instrument
he said he loved too much
to learn to play

Devastated

Next time, I'mma smack the taste
from their mouth
next time, I'm not going to
stay quiet, keep my thoughts to myself
or hold them in until
I'm as loud as sound will allow

next time, I will remember its name
I'll call her back
I'll tell invisibility it's impossible
next time I'll be seen, I'll be
restored, cherished and treasured
next time, I will be the champion
the one who stands at the top
of a journey, victoriously, next time I will

witness my greatness, call it by its name
when I walk past reflections, I will
answer that call, wake up early
push past my limits, limit my excuses
stop calling them limitations
the next time I doubt my own legend
I'll find letters from my students
call on my ghosts
let the depression laugh itself to sleep
the next time will be different
it won't be an old song on repeat
or wheels turning through mud, it won't
be the same old movie, it won't
earworm with an easy hook

next time, I won't call it
by my name

Endure

For those who allow vulnerability
after the first beer, or the second
blunt, or last call
for those who hold their emotions like fists
a balled-up childhood we swing, or
swig, or swallow away
you are not an anomaly, you're not
the odd one out, the runt of the litter
or a burden
you're not a bother, you're a brother
or a long-lost family member
waiting to be found
you're worth time, you're worth my time
and patience and understanding
you're worth taking
the higher road, or being the bigger person
you're not alone, no matter how absent
you feel from your smile, you are not alone
even when you're alone
after you've pushed the world
away with swinging hands, clawing
scratching for something to hold on to
when the depression answers all your calls
before you can reach the phone, still
there is someone or something that needs you
to stay, not just live, but thrive
not to suffer, but to be alive, in every way
they can't

you are a collection of decisions
made by forebears, you are more
than you know
more than doubt, than what you can't
expect or express
just be here and age, every moment, time
spent incubating, marinating
molding yourself
into gray hairs and good decisions
let your first choice be to stay
to love, to hold all that you are
like a snow globe placed on your mantle
for everyone to glimpse
for everyone to know
you're not done, not by a longshot
that the world tried
to end you, and you
survived

In Hail

Grit my teeth

breathe

open my eyes

breathe

shower
　clothes
　　breakfast
　　　calendar
　　　　clock
　　　　　keys
　　　　　　car

breathe

GPS
　delay
　　delay
　　　delay

breathe

the HOV lane, the impression of a parking lot
the exit I need, a Homeric excursion

empathy abandoned

breathe

thousands of cars
          one person
each

schedule
     a countdown until the next time I

breathe

into a keyboard
   dreams type

the future you want
to see, body tired, ache
from sleep deprived

students
       time
         machines

POs
    stopwatch
           OC warning

students
       mirrors

judges
    predators
         predictors
           policymakers

grit my teeth

breathe

too many questions for my questions
too many people, working hard to gatekeep the answers,
my dreams are full

of love, so much love
enough to keep my students safe
young eyes engulfed in pain
and we breathe, clench our fists
until palms bleed, our target is too large
too strong, too overwhelmingly right
too infallible, so we trick ourselves
into believing this pain
belongs to choice
and we hit, and we yell, and we fight so hard
hoping someone notices our bruises
hoping someone finds a way out
and will offer, just, time, to sit and breathe
maybe I can
be that person

when I breathe deep it's usually because
I dwelled on something I want to forget
I've tried to forget this hurt
this weighted gasp, the achy stomach
it feels like my breath knows me
better than I do
the quiet inhalation, then sharp exhale
it has no poker face, when I breathe deep
I'm angry, I'm emptied, I'm about to
explode, or let go
and this breath is my last hold
my barely-noticed pull
subconscious metronome of life

when I breathe deep
someone's cut me off in traffic
when I breathe deep
my rent is raised, but my paychecks are not
when I breathe deep
I remember my mother died

after I sent her last 4 calls to voicemail
and everything's been deleted

I'm constantly breathing deep
I'm constantly trying to suppress a voice
telling me to just fall apart and sleep for a month, or forever
but instead, I breathe
as deep as my lungs can hold
I try to take in as much air
as my chest will allow
until it hurts
until I hurt so bad, I forget
how bad I've hurt
until I forget
until I forget
until I
breathe

Self-Portrait

Strained reflection
you, smile like slingshot
laughter and an avalanche
gated grin always, unlocked
shelter in hugs. life
continuously in bloom. weathering doubt
of a belly more confident
than faded muscle
present and joyful

I Call Myself Back

Like a child playing from sunrise to sunset
smelling like summer and outside
like a missed moment
to show the footprints left behind
I call myself back
so that time spent moving forward
is not time spent forgetting
to give my heart a moment
to weep, to question the darkness
implanted in my family tree
I call myself back, because I've forgotten
too many times, letting trepidation run rampant
allowed depression too much
space at my table
told my misery, *wait until I'm alone*
then I'll allow myself to feel, to wear this hurt
like the old sweater it is and stop avoiding
the parts of my blooming
that singe the skin
I call myself back, to not forget the fire
how it may nourish, heal or devastate
I call myself back to the blight
relationships I've let cherry then smolder
to what I've watched simmer
listen to like rainfall
I don't hear or see, but know its arrival
by the smell, knowing everyone
is experiencing the same
downpour and we all see the lightning

we all feel the thunder, I hear it
calling me back, to moments neglected
calling myself back, like a dinner bell
calling me home, and learning to love
all of it

Human

Little collection, assembly of twinkles
stretching like stretchy things, baby blossom
hands of flower petals or puddles of lips
let me bumblebee your daytime to honey
let me lavender your sadness aromatherapy
how many planets have you locked away
in the past
destinations dying
as quickly as they're dreamt
tiny cloud of a person, shadow in the sky
casting more shade
than physically manifested
reading the braille of your touch
the rough patch covering some years
blushed with insecurity, tortured cotton candy
of a person
fussy chore, tangible ugly, like iniquity, you are
a sunrise, you, a harvest, the rest
after work, the reward in a gamble
the strut of self-assurance
after assessment, an answer
every answer, even the questions
baby ducks following tail by tail
baby *anythings* primed to absorb
and listen
and be loved
and become
love

Credo

Become the grinding and shift of growth
a bonsai unkempt

a blind wisdom tree
surviving forest fire alone

on a peak, a mariposa careless and plucked
from bustling beauty

I won't wait for a funeral
to embrace repute or ovation

I will love myself
the way I love others

I will forgive myself
as I have forgiven others

I will write the stories
my family has not, or will not write

I will live my mother's legacy,
one of her greatest works of art

I will breathe daily for my ancestors
calling on them for strength
living beyond disappointments

I will be patient with myself
as I am patient with others

I will accept what this universe gives me
without staring at its cracks

I will love the happy I find
I will call it by the names of family passed

no ax above my head enduringly waiting
no *I told you so* or bitter ego

only the hope I've held in daydreams
one by one, returning home to nest

Backscatter

Do I speak with love
or allow pain a nest to sleep, do I
close my spirit and become gray
with indignant resentment
who do I rely on now
consciousness is an enemy with unimpeachable memory
when my vision is dysmorphic
when clothing betrayed my confidence
and I am as breakable as a mirror
how do I mend this brittle boy
with a mangled man's sight
how do I love myself
as easily as I do anyone else
allow myself to trust myself
when the most vehement enemy
has my eyes

Making

Blood for the family I've lost
for the "family" thrown out
spoiled and unnecessary, blood
for the heart that pumps empathy
telling the world they are loved
that everyone needs and wants love
whether they know it or not, blood
for the times I sacrificed my joy
for someone else's wellbeing, for learning
a mentor's heart continuously breaks
and rebuilds itself
a phoenix daring
to articulate its suffering
sweat, for the mountains climbed

trying to find strength after loss
trying to find strength after loss
trying to find strength after loss
trying to find strength after loss

for the days my body feels
as heavy as my heart, and my limbs
won't move
as dark as days when leaving
the bed is the only victory
sweat for the work, because "easy" means
it wasn't worth it, because sweat won't come
unless it's worth it, let your determination
become drill sergeant, wiping
your brow, and carrying on

tears, for every day
for the seconds of clarity
the times I held back tears
like a cowardly dam, how masculinity
is the ghost town I am afraid will haunt me
how I'm afraid to drown in this sadness
now lives in the eyes
and everyone is hurting, and you can see it
when they introduce themselves,
how no one allows time
to mourn and learn then grow
how crying doesn't always feel like healing
how nothing feels more present than breaking down
tears for our juvenescence
my god, the most lost and underappreciated
how most times we only needed
a pat on the back, a hug, or anyone insisting
it's good, it's all good
you can let it out
you can let it go

Albuquerque 2005

We took the third longest tramway in operation
to the top of the Sandia Crest
just her and I, a quiet ride
the peeks climbing over the horizon like
some giant sleeping beast raising from sleep

> *seventeen and all I wanted to do*
> *was borrow your rental*
> *and do hoodrat shit with my*
> *friends*

the trolley was heaving, people of every type
phones and cameras trying to steal away
the moment in snapshots for later
proof to their friends, they were here
others murmured prayers for safety
in an attempt to cull their discomposure
but you were calm, no fear, no distress
not sure if you looked out the window
not sure if I did either
you are the important part
I wanted to remember now, you, the only site
worth seeing, at the peak we spilled out
like water from a burning house
I went for a hike
left you to take in the view alone
you loved the mountains
you loved life, and I don't
remember the hike, I don't
remember the parties, or friends

I don't remember the poetry, but I remember you
tired, too hurting to walk with me, but enough
strength to summit with your son
it's hard to appreciate the beauty
of your surroundings when you're a kid
you don't know only 12 years remains
and every second with her matters
when you're a child
you'll think the mountains to remember
and forget your mother's smile
someday too soon
you'll know the view was never the point
one day you'll be older
you'll summit the Sandia Crest again
and on that peak, on every peak
she'll be there, waiting, smiling
watching, you
as the most beautiful landscape
on God's green earth

575 4 Loss

I miss my mother
I miss the mountain, one day
I'll visit them both

angel, with angels
heaven on top of a desert
mother's gift

regretting all the moments
I spent selfishly
wishing for more time

too many wasted
chances to help her
God, give me a time machine

I can no longer
think of ending my own life
I live for her now

After

Some days, you're a decrepit home
a house assembled to burn, walls ablaze
no one can walk through, or out of
or away from
a scorching city, some days
you're a lake, dried and lifeless
only salt to prove you ever existed
some days asking
for an exit sign, if now is a good time to go
or wait for the ocean to swell into a scream
anger like catastrophe, cataclysm
like something alive and out
of control, almost a mistake
almost an apology, all most misery
and the oxygen taken to feed it
mistakes becoming kindled, fuel
when all you wanted was warmth
holding whatever survives
like a family treasure
in the embers
of a decrepit home

All I Ever Wanted

The warmth of her smile

        behind a wall of fear, I've known

to carry joy like a kettle

        an empty spot anticipating, a dream

telling my beautiful to wait

        doubts of a family existing

    until

tears too perfect to hold

        the dagger behind my eyes

believe happiness will last

        forever
        become the only weapon I fear

exactly like it should

        whatever is meant to be will be

we shine like a grinning child

        tumbling like the gift of growing

our shelter in a storm

                                    the family I always wanted

shivering with questions of

                                    once prayed for doubt like

how do I function without

                                    a broken thing leaving

                love, like canvas to brush

Editor's Notes

87

No matter where you are
know someone is smiling
there is a heart and hug
all the captured parts of beauty
I'm glad you let yourself become
a garden
a place where everyone's
invited

Come Into This

I come into peace like how I imagine
some families come into money, over time
or when someone passes away
or passes information, "game"
like a golden ticket to more golden tickets

I've come into peace like I'm visiting
a museum in my hometown, a mansion turned menagerie
I've come into peace as a tourist, like
I'm only welcome on Tuesdays
when I can use my eyes for free
when I can write my voice like music notes
and play a song of thoughts
I've come into peace
exhausted from knocking
drained from giving
          all I have
to finally be allowed to come into peace
money is not the answer
but that's usually the only one I hear from
those who've held it so freely
those who've misplaced cash
and never feared the uproot
I've come into peace thinking
I needed too much before I could hold it
before I could walk through a door of content
and call myself home. call myself a custodian of all the clutter
and detritus of my life
call myself earning peace instead of having it

grandfathered to my anxiety
finding peace where my parents did not
finding peace when all I've seen is struggle
finding peace like cotton candy in a hurricane
I've come into the peace I've claimed
building it out of rent
and things I don't own
learning to live on a tilted foundation
and calling it home, calling it mine
peace, and claiming it for every descendant

My Own Words

Don't do anything I wouldn't do
but if you do
name it after me

don't fear your greatness
but if you do, make shelter
in your darkness, make a home
out of the fear you wear
like a seasonal coat

I define myself
a grilled cheese and tomato soup-type
comfort, like remembering
my mother's perfume when
all I can say is, *I'm sorry* or *I love you*
the opening of arms
the closing of an embrace
all I can say is, *good morning* or *good night*
when the torment is only tears
and your moments are always years
and all you know is rust, I'll be
like, *you good bro. you gotta get up bro*
you gotta move and move
and let your motion
be the revolution you need
to call yourself love and
live through the darkness you thought
only held your demons

Fool's Gold

I hide myself
beneath fictitious treasure

a holiday seldom celebrated
where hurt drips like
tree sap my heart's forest

one day those who cut, will
take what can no longer hold itself
take the debris of my loss
all that becomes weight

turn kite in the wind
let go of my kettlebells of regret
reclaim what was, before
possibility was tainted
by fear of what might be

again, or never, with both arms
stretched to smother the sky
I won't let doubt ground me
letting my shoulders lead
instead of leading the ground
let my knees bend only when climbing

when it's time to fly
let my voice be cotton in a gust
let doubt become terrified to exist
at the heights I climb
what I might find, and how

no one can come with me
in this journey to love myself better

when it's time to fly
I won't question
if anyone has ever done this
won't silence my gut
waiting for a sign
when it has already flown away
with its head tilted to the side
wondering if I'll follow

Pericardium

My heart be hoover dam
be a standing ovation
be an encore
a showstopper, my heart
be a levee, a construction zone
for unsolicited advice, a self-serving
single use, coffee cup, my heart be
calloused, be hands, be my father's
hands, be the bend
in my mother's knees, and back
be a bed, leaned upon until God
or time shouldered her last breath, my heart
be fractured, be a broken place
held in place like windshield
my heart be a shield, be a sword
with only pointed ends
be pointing me out in the crowd
of my temper, be a lighthouse
in my torment, my heart be fear
hesitating and skipping
a murmur of what I really want to say, be saying so much
with only pulse, a yellow light
in a city running late
my heart be a heaven, be a doorway
be an opening
be the only way out, be taking everything
be bundled
together like firewood, only a few degrees away from inferno
my heart be a ribbon, a ribbon-cutting, a cut

from the editor's floor, my heart be
behind the scenes
of every scene, a Blu-ray bonus
a director's veto saying
no, this has to stay, this part
needs to stay

Unspoken

Home
is an inkless typewriter
begging restoration
demanding a story
every home
becoming a rusted lineage
a family forest forgotten
in the plow and grind
of surviving

home
is a locked door
a thing we keep in
the family
a bundling or kindling
bound so tight
so unwatered
it is practically
smoke

On My Back

I carry my home with me
like the turtle, my wife, I am,
I lumber and curl and unroll myself through
a universe of strawberries or mangos or other things
that are awesome to watch a sulcata eat

maybe we're all our own tiny oasis
maybe we're just a few drops of rain from
calling ourselves a river
I carry my home wherever I am
like I ain't just my trauma, a truth
I won't allow myself to have, *because*
and put a period behind
the things we don't intend to revisit

my demons feed on cynicism
like hands around my throat, but I don't
really give them the time
these days, I built a beautiful home
in my chest
in the people I clutch and the life that grasps me in return

sometimes, I want and want and the
hopelessness becomes a buzzing
the world still has a million holes to fall through
and I don't have answers to save anyone
just a home I can quiet my panic
enough room to water my solace

Third and Dena

In the river of my chest,
only my heart floats, only
my voice allows anchor, an encore
for all that has yet to ornament
a story to tell in the flow of my rapids
grabbing for anything named refuge

I dream of my mother and I find myself
missing everything before it's gone
like the punchline, or sleep,
or love, or people
in my dreams, I'm in the home I grew up in
a skyscraper daring me to fly
the message in a sturdy branch to stand
or pull me from a hurricane's storm surge
pretending to be a child, screaming
through the yard
circling my childhood home, a flickering
light, an underwater promise
traveling faster without air

Catalyst

The world begins at the joints,
the parts of the body that move and
dance and find rhythm in drums,
carve guitars out of trees and find a way
to turn a groan of sorrow into chamber music

the world begins with a child's laughter or
the moments after an argument or
when an understanding crawls its way from
the need to be right, the world begins
when it ends for someone you love

the loss of a part of you is like
losing color from sight, how the world looks
the same for everyone, but
somehow you no longer see the rainbows,
the emptiness creating room

is continuously beginning,
begging for moments
to live like the mountains
and find herself eternal and immoveable

Honor This Feeling

Time, is a tricky demon
as if not moving at all until creeping
into a deadline, or relative, time is the fear
mother, birthing anxieties we're years from
unpacking in therapy sessions
a family *cycle* could never afford

I was 20 years into life before
writing a 5-year plan
am I behind or advanced in my own judgment
time is the one in the backseat screaming
telling me, I've equaled, failure

what have I, what am I doing now
like a head-on collision, time asks,
why, and *what for*
and to prove, to explain
yourself and show your work
and where you've been and why
your creativity is
hot air balloon, too depressed
to get off the ground
time is saying, *you're too far gone*
you're too almost
empty, you're a risk, and *why push now*
when you have so little time, sometimes
I sit and think, and breathe, watch the sky, and
kiss the sun and maybe

that is enough

when all my bones are dust

and all that is love is

Hollow

If my words were a bird
they'd be a quiet owl
nothing to gawk at
clipped wings and not even noticed
standing perched
at the intersection of opinions
balanced effortlessly between listening
and waiting to explode, at times
words were the preamble violence
fists swinging like the ring of a bell
often and at the beginning of my learning
I learned to use my words
to fly me a million miles from hurt
an ocean away from hating myself and
across the country from doubt
I give this feather
I take flight
my wings
my song
whispered

Praise

The distance we close in moments
the time it takes to go
from thought to action, the will
the restraint and knowing our bodies
are capable

praise be the mornings
when the earth cools itself
ready for the day or bloody from night
praise be the days I miss my mother
the everyday, the grief holding on like
the last part of her in my life, praise be
the health, the decisions
based around the heart
the lighthouse of emotional navigation
at times guiding you to the reefs
praise be the seconds I take myself seriously
the morning commutes
built like a confessional
for the eyes
and the desert of unlearning
that keeps them

If Only

Imagine
this is the year
when you remove our ego
the year people care
about our children
give wings to dreams
and honestly try
to help each other
imagine a world
that only wants you healthy
perhaps
this is the year
we adjust, perhaps
this is the year
we learn our own
smiles

Welcome Home

Where you are loved
this shelter, is it real, or still
becoming, redemption
for parts of yourself yet forgiven
do you need to be forgiven to feel
welcomed, is a home held hostage to regret
has your construction stopped
or are you still an unsaid sentence
are you complete, do you feel yourself rising
further from grounded

is humbling yourself a chore or a choir
have you acquired anything
that matters more than money
like a personality, sense of humor, or empathy

this place, at times, is lazy, so corny
I want to grab my entire species and shake
the fear out of them, destroying beauty
an entire universe on the same cycle
of live and die, telling me nothing lasts
including anger
after you confront it, but if you can just stop
being a weirdo, for a moment
maybe we'd all find a bit more
hope, that's all I really want, maybe that's all
anyone wants, hope, the opportunity
to think, *this might get better*
this might not suck forever, a blessing

a bomb we're convinced was a time capsule
capturing euphoria from venting
our grisly in a trauma or photo dump
working for unattainable rent in the afterlife
hoping the world remembers the things
we never got the chance
to finish but imagined
so real it became a memory, false
and I get tired and fold inward
anyway, welcome
home, please remove
your shoes

Desensitized

I see myself falling
sometimes,
like a slow drift, a comfortable descent
I see myself
at my highest and the golden glow I emit
light like a power source, I see myself
powerful and imagine the exhaustion
discipline to avoid apathy for a world
intent to burn itself to the ground
like everyone I know, the denial of demise,
thinking maybe if I can tame and grasp
universal appreciation, I see
the good I could do, the good I'm doing
wonder where I could be with limits left
unchecked, and doubt starving in the attic
I see myself a book afraid to read myself
procrastination as a life choice
attempting to extend moments to days
thinking I can outsmart my
ancestors holding my wrists
like being shackled to a cloud and
too tired to wake
up, I see too much,
sorrow like colors and every day
a dead rainbow, I see so many
stewing in their fury
a few degrees from bubbling over

these days, I don't find myself

scared of serial killers
psychotic clowns, or
ghosts I can't apologize to
my fear exists in everyday folk
less than a thousand dollars away
from kicking in their neighbors' door
I'm scared
of the power going out and the gates to our animal
ripping through the reasons holding us sane
I'm scared we're all grieving, all in denial
bleeding hearts angry no one sees
us polling, together or
alone, I see myself there, too
I see what good I could do
and how in doing so I could lose
everything I am, and all my joy is thrown
over my shoulder. tossed like a dandelion,
a prayer seen true, as long as
you don't care where it lands

Poet

I see you
ad-libbing your life
you've gone
off script, write out your thoughts
the incremental steps, your stories
the tickets, the currency, a current moving
through a mudslide, too much debris
not enough time to filter an ocean
asking, *are these tears*
holding your sadness like desalination
there is so much ocean in you, most
is raging, dehydrated, dehumanized, degiveafucked
I see you, wilting the days away, waiting
for an email or gig to book, waiting
for your book to finish itself
enlisting help and still finding
ways to sneak a kick to self, I see you
little brown boy never grown man
I see you child locked in optimism
seeing good in everyone but your own
shortcomings, wondering,
when's your comeback
everyone's wondering if you'll come back
or set yourself adrift
in a stream of unconsciousness
we see you, the ancestors are watching
they aren't as worried about you as you are
they see time tangible

they're holding onto the good times
the moments past
and yet to come, seeing you yet to come
arriving at a party planned for you, I see you
we all do
you're not hiding,
I promise you're not
invisible

Immigrant

After Alberto Rios

The border is banana flavored candy
it's licorice, it's spoiled
milk, clumpy, and sour, calling
itself cheese, saying it makes
my sandwich better
calling my pb&j unwelcomed
it calls from unknown numbers at 7 am
and says someone is stealing my credit
it says I don't have credit with them
says my mother owes them money
and they want it from her grave
it calls again at 9 am
says it's on east coast time
says it's on its own time, then calls
from different unblocked numbers
the border is pushy
needy, always acting out for attention
always off-task or
turns in assignments late or not at all
the border's parents came in
for a teacher conference
the border's mother is confused
doesn't understand why we make her
child out to be such a nuisance
says, *at home around our people
the border is the life of the party,* cleans up
after itself and is never disrespectful to her
the border's father didn't show up

the border's father is drunk at a bar
in the afternoon, trying to forget
trying to figure out ways to build a border
around his border, trying to understand his
child. tonight, he'll go home to the border
in his chest
wake the border out of its rest
make it dance
the border's father will say things
like, *do that trick I taught you, do it*
make everyone disappear
make everyone feel so unseen
that they vanish from our sight
the border knows many tricks, many
scams, its parents were grifters, swindlers
the border wants to be something more
something different, but it's the same ol' impasse
doesn't change or know if it can
so, its sunrises and sunsets become children
and it watches them dance
for a secret hour every day

Untitled

The time has come
arrived when requested
tracking number, scheduled
alert, the time has come, it's here
asking for water or where the bathroom is
or what kind of tea you have, an uninvited but
predicted guest, as an ill-tempered gush
of tears, a clenched jaw or fingers rolled
tight like grief

the time has come and it wants its due, asking for rent, it
came as white blood cells chewing
the life out of my family, it arrived as
a humid heavy depression denial
the trauma family will never
acknowledge

it pulled up
as imposter
syndrome, it came
in the moments my life could
have changed, the time has come
to step into all I can be but my knees
feel weak, I'm not sure if I'm strong enough
to practice what I preach, I just want to be
the best version of me, a sample of free
air I can breathe, where I can breathe
without anxiety

Little Prayer

Tiny hope, mured
whispered through a dream

I pray the elote man comes by
today, I hope his hands are rested
pray he brings home his life
and livelihood, for his family.
I pray gas goes down,
pray the family in my building isn't waiting
till next month to fix the work truck
I been said prayers for the family
found myself on concrete
praying life into a vehicle
I pray for enough
enough energy to make it through
the day, a little prayer for the chicken to thaw
fast enough to calm the raging in our bellies
prayed for the check to look right
prayed the gas tank a liar
prayed for miles and at times was answered
stranded on the road, still
the baby prayer, a tiny lil' homie
of hope, I pray for tiny
victories for all my homies
infinite accomplishments
something I can hold
like a participation trophy, at least I'm here
and I pray that is
enough

Angry at America While Visiting Cuba

I know a kid raised on family trauma
believing in the suffering of grandparents
seeing his grandmother's faith as blind
a homeland turned horror show, I know
a country named hypocrisy, calling itself great, daring its
people to deny it, spitting
on the rest of the world
trying to drown a dash
in the middle of an ocean
I know a place where healthcare is free
where everyone has a home
but places buckets to catch the rain, still
building a hospital instead of a wall, asking
its people to resemble the ocean they wade in
to rise and fall with the weather, to trust
until home is a harvest
knowing the starvation is not stagnation
no pointing finger, but raised fist, if you knew
me you would know the tears
my father holds in his doubt
the legacy fading
into the gray in his memories
you would know the "Cuban" I became
when the United States divorced me
from my own identity
how I learned to fold

myself into what others told me I was
how all I knew became nothing to know
how we unlearn as we grow, how we unravel
as we learn

I know a kid so confused
so sad and so hurt and so and so and
so many words that cannot be translated
how I was transatlantic before
transferring funds
how a dollar could mean life or a curled fist
how my ancestors have the same hands
but mine are so much softer
when the heat speaks to my body
I am baptized in perspiration
I am bathed in perspective
I am 5 years old watching Pablo filet a shark
with bullet holes in his arms and chest
I become a story turned fairytale
testimony turned to lie
and all the anger it births
the unsettling from resetting, the negro
Enrique Lewis tried to beat out of my mother
the white my father never felt
anywhere but his knuckles
if you knew this place, you would
love this place
burn out the white supremacy
holding a knee, or knife, or gun, to the neck
of a family I'll never know, a *big brother* bully
watching you like the fuckup they never claim to be
America the fake, land of the overdraft fee
home of the slave, genocide the braves
bent on saving nothing but a buck
a bronco not even native to people annihilated
or incinerated or alienated
pushed so far back

until forgotten, my hands are shaking
I'm holding a pen like a hand
grenade or a handgun
I'm pointing at myself, hoping anyone is struck
enlightened, hoping I'm not stuck frightened
too small and too fearful
to raise my hand and call bullshit
to a room of hypocrites
wrapped in stars, and drenched
in my ancestors' blood

Demands

I've come into this place
to fuck shit up
to shake the dust off the drone
of another day
I've come to be heard and seen
but only after I've listened
I've listed out my grievances
I've attached meeting notes with power
and bullet points, I've made a point
to name my demons, they all look
like a cringe expression, they all have the same hairs
standing at attention the moment a guillotine drops
I'm done being kind, people haven't been that
since Blockbusters and VCRs anyway
I'm done being angry
or passive, or passionate, I just want to be breaking news or
breaking cycles, or somewhere
between yelling poems and setting off homemade explosives
to the nearest financial institution
I've come into this
poem to release, to find comfort in no longer
holding frustration like a smallpox blanket
to quiet the wailing of my grief
in hyperbole, wearing a smile
like the mask of the kid who died
when his mother did, I've come
to a resting place
where the grass is the greenest and always
gets the best sunlight

and a full share of water

Catholicon

Come one come all
let me tell you about this joy
batteries sold separately
it can mold itself
into any part of your day
taking you from dookie to truly
blessed, the best
my answer key to life's mess

it's the cowabunga of my mother
running in the rain after watching Ninja Turtles
it's watching her slip and fall
my siblings and I giving all our air to laughter
this joy laughs at pain
thinking it has a place in this memory
this joy is automatic, systematic,
hydromatic, hell, literal lightning
grease sold separately

this joy tells me
money doesn't matter tonight
while planning Ivanna's funeral
it's Jiminy Glick the day after she passed
a giggle forced from the gut of grief
but this joy is now

this joy is being sold in fancy boutiques
for the price of a house, it's shutting down
trafficking of everything but love of any kind
it's broke, but not broken

this joy is a find, a light
in the darkest places of the mind

this joy is for the oppressed
spaces, gaunt faces without the luxury
to pretend or fake it till you make it
this joy is naked, and raw, and real
and tangible, and obtainable
standing right behind the obstacles
strange but familiar on the page
it's coming to a city near you
you won't find it in stores, supplies will last
as long as devils persist, as long as ancestors
allow us to refuel

this joy is included
in every bad memory
even the ones yet to come
a must have gift
a legacy, a trust, my descendants
can rely on
even with batteries
sold separately
this joy still leaves
the lights on

Author

Matthew 'Cuban' Hernandez is a poet, emcee, speaker, actor, and performance coach from Jacksonville, Florida. He has toured as far as Abu Dhabi and nearly every major city in the United States and Europe, performing, teaching and coaching poetry. A teaching artist for over 15 years, Matthew has spent the last 10 years working in youth detention centers across Los Angeles County, currently serving as the Director of Juvenile Programming for Street Poets, Inc. In addition, he is a current Lead Teacher and Co-Founder of Spoken Literature Art Movement. Cuban has opened for artists such as Wu-Tang, performed for platforms such as BuzzFeed and NPR and even appeared on the award-winning television show, Better Things. Matthew is also a three-time Southern Fried poetry slam champion and an award-winning poetry coach. Cuban's favorite activity is making people feel great; sometimes he does this through hip hop and poetry.

Artist

Born in Richmond, Virginia, Robalu Gibsun is a multidisciplinary artist and educator. He graduated from Virginia Commonwealth University's Communication Arts department and has had his art and poetry published in various journals. As a TEDxRVA Speaker, Southern Fried Poetry Slam Champion, and *Verses and Flow* Poet, Gibsun advocates for authenticity and fearless creativity.

Founded by Matt Sedillo and David A. Romero, El Martillo Press publishes writers whose pens strike the page with clear intent; words with purpose to pry apart assumed norms and to hammer away at injustice. El Martillo Press proactively publishes writers looking to pound the pavement to promote their work and the work of their fellow pressmates. El Martillo is the builder of bridges and the destroyer of walls.

El Martillo Press titles:

- *All Brown Boys Get Trumpets* by Matthew 'Cuban' Hernandez
- *Chimeras Dream on Barren Lands* by Alex Alpharaoh
- *Paper Birds: Feather by Feather / Pájaros de papel: pluma por pluma* by Sonia Gutiérrez
- *Blackout* by Anna Lombardo
- *detoxification of the body* by gabor g. gyukics
- *WE STILL BE: Poems and Performances* by Paul S. Flores
- *Touch the Sky* by Donato Martinez
- *the daughterland* by Margaret Elysia Garcia
- *Yo soy Romero* by David A. Romero

To purchase these books and to keep up with new titles, visit elmartillopress.com.

www.ingramcontent.com/pod-product-compliance
Lightning Source LLC
Chambersburg PA
CBHW072240150726
48002CB00005B/2180